KU-009-253

Victorian and Edwardian
SUFFOLK
from old photographs

1   Men of the Suffolk Yeomanry at Manor Farm, Henham Hall Park, 1910

2   The Southwold fishing fleet returned to harbour with the herring catch, *c.* 1890

Victorian and Edwardian

SUFFOLK

from old photographs

Introduction and commentaries by

COLIN HARRISON

B. T. BATSFORD LTD
LONDON

To Rhoda, Tommy, and Pip

COUNTY COPY

First published 1973
Text © Colin Harrison 1973
ISBN 0 7134 0126 5
Printed in Great Britain by
William Clowes & Sons Limited
London, Beccles and Colchester
for the publishers B. T. Batsford Ltd
4 Fitzhardinge Street, London W1H 0AH

HERTFORDSHIRE
COUNTY LIBRARY
942.64
5798314

3 One of the side-lines at this tannery in Combs was the manufacture of leather belting. Much of it would be used on the mechanised harvesting machines that were being introduced all over the county, *c*. 1899

CONTENTS

Acknowledgments 6

Introduction 7

ILLUSTRATION NUMBER

The County Towns 7–26

The Rural Scene 27–42

Royal Occasions 43–48

Getting About 49–75

The Common Man 76–89

In Days of Sail   90–102

High Days and Holidays   103–113

At Work   114–127

Disaster   128–137

In Public Service   138–142

Sports, Pastimes and Seaside   143–158

Round About Suffolk   159–170

ACKNOWLEDGMENTS

I would like to thank the following for their generous help in locating photographs and permitting me to use them in this book: the staff of Abbot's Hall Museum, Stowmarket (1, 3, 17–19, 23–26, 28–31, 33–35, 37, 38, 40, 42, 51–57, 62, 65–66, 69–71, 74, 76, 80, 82, 84–86, 93, 99–101, 103, 105, 106, 108, 110, 113–116, 118, 125, 132, 134, 135, 138, 141, 143–147, 149–151, 154, 157, 159, 162–165, 167–170). The museum, which houses the Suffolk Photographic Survey, displays something in the order of 4,500 objects including waggons, drills, ploughs and other farm implements, passenger vehicles, craft tools and domestic utensils. A visit is recommended to all who have an interest in Suffolk and East Anglia. The Librarian and staff of the Bury St Edmunds Public Library (7, 8, 10, 11, 13, 14, 43, 45, 78, 87, 88, 112, 121, 128); Mr M. P. Statham and the Bury St Edmunds and West Suffolk Record Office (4); Mr M. Canham; Mr W. Serjeant and the East Suffolk Record Office (15, 16, 20–22, 124); Mr O. G. Jarman and the Jarman Collection (5, 44, 47, 48, 73, 77, 89, 119, 140, 148); the Librarian and staff of the Lowestoft Public Library (58, 60, 63, 79, 92, 96–98, 111, 120, 126, 127, 133, 142, 152, 153, 155, 156, 159, 166); The Vick Collection, Ipswich and East Suffolk Record Office (137, 139); West Suffolk Newspapers Ltd; West Suffolk Record Office (27, 32, 36, 39, 41, 49, 50, 68, 72, 75, 81, 83, 102, 104, 109, 117, 122, 123, 130, 131, 136, 160). Photographs 12, 67, 161 come from the Publisher's collection.

Finally, I would like to thank the many individuals – too many to name here – who willingly gave their time to talk to me about the life and times of Victoria and Edward.

4 A punt on the pond at the Grange, Chelsworth. Mr G. R. Pocklington, editor of the *Boys' Own Paper* helped to build the craft. Photograph taken 7 June 1911

INTRODUCTION

Suffolk, the most eastern of English counties, and one of the largest with an area of 1,481 sq. miles, is surrounded on three sides by land in the form of Norfolk, Cambridge, and Essex, while the North Sea is its eastern-most barrier. Its name, which comes from the Saxon appellation of 'Sudfolk', dates from the fifth century. The population increased steadily during the nineteenth century, from 214,000 in 1801 to 337,000 in 1851 and reaching 384,000 in 1901.

It is a flat county, the highest point being at Rede which reaches only some 420 feet above sea level. This general evenness, taken together with the strong loam soil which covers all but the coastal belt, produces excellent crops and accounts for the bias towards agriculture that is obvious even today, and appears clearly in so many of the photographs in this collection. In 1804 Suffolk was considered 'one of the best cultivated counties in England'. Certainly it was one of the first to cease the old practice of leaving fields fallow once in three years, and by the early years of Queen Victoria's reign all the county had gone over to a six-yearly cycle of cropping. This involved wheat, barley, turnips, oats, clover (for use as hay), and the land was then grazed and ploughed for wheat again. In the west wheat predominated as did barley in the east.

Much of the barley crop was, and is today, used for malting in the production of beer. My first introduction to this county, many years ago, took the form of the riddle: 'Where does Tolly Cobbold face the Greene Knight in mortal combat?' The answer lies on the inn signs that abound in each of the county's 500 villages – they are of course the main beer suppliers in Suffolk.

Although fading from the scene during the later Victorian and Edwardian period the growth of flax and hemp had been an important element in shaping the social life of the county: 'Suffolk hempen cloth' was once well known the nation over. Attempts, all unavailing,

5   A cricket group at Ampton Hall, *c.* 1910

were made during Victoria's time to revive this industry, but its place was taken by such textiles as sailcloth; coconut fibres; horsehair; and clothing.

Until the coming of the motor car at the turn of the century, Suffolk relied upon the horse for almost all of its power (wind and water provided the rest) and developed one of the most famous of shire horses – the Suffolk Punch. Sad to record, but as the later photos show, the tractor and traction engine have now replaced the horse.

Cattle are, however, still to be found in plenty and Suffolk cows are highly regarded as milk producers. In 1840 the county managed to ship 40,000 firkins of butter to London.

Much of Suffolk's industry grew up during the reigns of Queen Victoria and King Edward and it remains, as it started, firmly based in manufacturing for agriculture. The other great source of employment was the fishing industry, which has its own section in the book. Centred upon Lowestoft, the fleets caught (and still do) mainly herring and mackerel, off the coast, but they were also seen in the far distant waters of Iceland after the cod and ling. They also developed a large trade in fish with Flanders across the channel.

However, the sea has not always been so kind to Suffolk. The coast-

6   The inmates of the Infirmary at Bury St Edmunds being taken for an outing, c. 1895

line which is some 50 miles long, is particularly prone to erosion, and over the centuries large parts of the coast have been eaten up by the action of the waves. Some of the photographs here show examples of this occurring. They illustrate the kind of action that has led to the almost total extinction of the village of Dunwich.

Suffolk is used to trouble, in fact it has been in one sort of trouble or another since the dawn of history, what with invasions, rebellions and revolutions. None of these has dampened the spirit of the people – this shines through the pages of this book. Suffolk was, and is, alive and well; today just as in Victorian times it is facing the modern world with eagerness.

This book reflects Suffolk during the reigns of Victoria and Edward, a period when photography was still a modern invention. The photographs the Victorians and Edwardians took reflect what they thought important and interesting, so we see them as they saw themselves, sometimes flatteringly, sometimes warts and all.

THE COUNTY TOWNS

For administrative purposes the county is divided into three parts: West Suffolk centred upon Bury St Edmunds, East Suffolk based upon Ipswich, and the borough of Ipswich. There are accordingly not one but two county towns, each with its own character and atmosphere.

BURY ST EDMUNDS

Described by Thomas Carlyle (1795–1881) as 'a prosperous brisk town, beautifully diversifying, with its clear brick houses, ancient clean streets, and twenty or fifteen thousand souls, the general grassy face of Suffolk' – a description typical then of the agricultural side of the county's nature.

At this time the town covered some 3,040 acres, being a mile-and-a-half by one-and-a-quarter. The population grew from 7,986 in 1811 to 12,538 in 1841, reflecting the early warning of agricultural unrest that was to boil over in 1874 in the strike and lock-out and the general movement away from the land to the towns.

7   The Buttermarket, Bury St Edmunds, *c.* 1890

Rapid development of the town was hindered by poor communication: the river Lark was only navigable to Fornham, a mile away, and the railway was a little late in arriving. The settlement of a dispute between the commissioners looking after the river Lark and the Corporation of the town did lead to the improvement of the river in the late 1880s. (see photo 48).

The central point of the town is the Abbey, built to house the remains of King Edmund of East Anglia. They were brought to the town in 903. In 1020 King Canute established a group of Benedictine monks here, and by 1032 a stone church had replaced the wooden one. Late in the eleventh century Abbot Baldwin began a larger church. Entrance to the Abbey was through the Great Gate; this was destroyed in 1327 following a rising by the people of the town – they were made to re-build it.

The town has been visited by many royal persons, but one of the most interesting reminders of the royal connection with the town is a window in the great church of St Mary which was given by Queen Victoria, together with marble round the nearby tomb, given by Edward VII, in commemoration of Mary Tudor, Queen of France, who died in Westhorpe in 1533 and had her remains re-interred here after the dissolution.

8 The Buttermarket, Bury St Edmunds, being used for a real market in 1890. A traditional ice-cream stall can be seen in the bottom right-hand corner

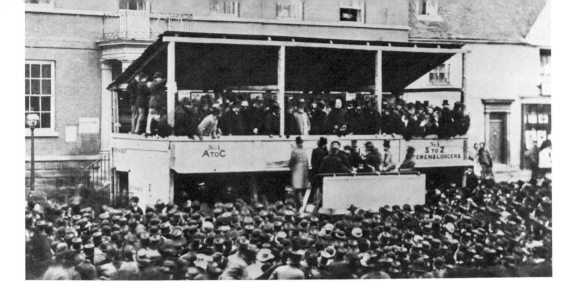

9 The first news picture taken in Bury St Edmunds (1868). This view of the 'hustings' was taken outside the Angel Hotel by Spanton. He tied the camera to a lamp post to hold it steady during the four seconds it took the wet plate to record the picture

10 Bury St Edmunds. The finale scene of the 1907 pageant which has been held in the Abbey gardens for many years. This pageant depicts the setting which holds it, for the Abbey was founded in 903 to hold the body of King Edmund of East Anglia who had been killed by the Danes some 33 years earlier at Hoxne. Bishop Theodred founded the first Abbey church to honour the memory of the saintly King who would not give up his faith to save his life. In 1214 the barons met at the high altar to take the solemn oath that led to their forcing King John to grant the freedoms in the Magna Carta

11 Bury St Edmunds: the staff outside Ridley's shop in 1890. The modern visitor will find that little has changed as far as this shop exterior is concerned

12 Eastgate Street, Bury St Edmunds, c. 1910. The east gate is now a thing of the past but this charming street is otherwise little changed

13 Bury St Edmunds in 1870: the corner of Guildhall and Westgate Streets, showing a typical butcher's shop whose design had changed little since medieval times

14 The inside of the Corn Exchange, Bury St Edmunds, *c.* 1909

15 Westgate Street, Ipswich, in 1859. This daguerrotype (the first practical process for producing photographs) was taken by Mr W. Thompson. The attractive buildings on the right have now made way for the building of a bank

IPSWICH

Ipswich, perhaps the real county town of Suffolk, lies at the estuary of the river Orwell and has been a flourishing seafaring place since Anglo-Saxon times.

During the 1700s it lost its great cloth industry, but being ideally situated for commerce it rose rapidly in wealth, population and importance during Victorian and Edwardian times. The population grew from 11,000 in 1801 to 25,000 in 1843 and 34,000 in 1861. The increasing flow of industry into the town attracted the lower paid workers from the farms. Perhaps the most notable of the people in this industrialisation was Robert Ransome, maker of all kinds of agricultural implements, whose name is still nationally recognised today.

16 Built at a cost of £4,250 in 1844 the New Customs House
dominates the dock at Ipswich. We see it as it looked in 1890

With increasing trade it became necessary to improve the sea-links with the rest of
Britain and indeed the rest of Europe, and the new docks were opened in 1842. This new
dock had a wet surface of 32 acres, with a depth of fourteen feet. But even this was not
enough and soon the railway reached the town and from 1846 the future of the area was
assured. By 1900 the population had reached 66,000 making it by far the largest town in
the county.

But we must not go away with the impression that Ipswich is in any way a drab town,
for the Suffolk countryside is never far away and creeps into the fringes of the town in
most pleasant ways.

17 Ipswich. Work in progress, *c.* 1900, at the top of Northgate Street in preparation for the re-making of the road with wooden paving

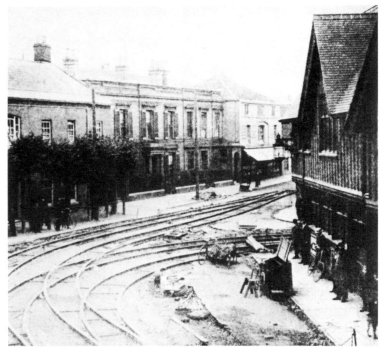

19 Major's Corner, Ipswich. The final stages of the laying of the tracks for the coming electric trams, 1902

18 *(below)* Ipswich, the picture outside the railway station about 1904

21 Carr Street, Ipswich in the early morning of 1888. Its name means a place where water flows, and until a few years before this photograph a stream followed Carr and Brook Streets to find its way down into the Wash

20 St Mary at Elms, Ipswich, c. 1890. These quaint cottages, once sought after by artists from all over East Anglia have now been pulled down

22 The corner pawn shop at St Mary Elms, Ipswich, in 1890. It has long since made way for other buildings

23 Ipswich Barracks, *c.* 1863. The guns are muzzle loaders of the style used during the Crimean War

24 Christchurch Park, Ipswich, 1903

25 Ipswich. The old cattle market seen in 1909

RURAL SCENE

A skyline dotted with giant elms, tall ripe corn cut by footpaths that are themselves guarded by the ever-present stiles and bounded by thick hedges. Scattered, as if by some giant's hand, the occasional farmhouse tucks itself into the corner of the picture. It all looks so calm and peaceful, but the scent of change is in the air. No longer can the ox regard himself as the chief motive power of the field; men grown old and weathered by their constant attendance upon nature are having to make way for the 'new fangled' machines. The nearby towns, where these mechanical aids are built, grow in size and at the expense of the skilled farmers and countrymen who are attracted to them by the higher wages.

Some jobs, however, are still for man alone and in the sheep dipping we see the traditional interdependence of animal and man.

Yes, in spite of the coming change, Suffolk was still a largely rural community and its splendour is nowhere better typified than in the eternal beauty of the works of its two famous painters – Gainsborough and Constable. In our photograph we see Flatford Bridge much as Constable must have viewed it.

27 Rattlesden. The traditional harvesting method – a scything team, c. 1895.

28 (overleaf) A rare photograph of oxen being used to harrow the ground at Theberton, c. 1885

26 Culpho. Putting down tile drains on Abbey Farm, c. 1900

29 Beating the bounds at Hasketon in 1887. On the extreme left is Col. Barlow with the map of the parish, while the gentleman with the tall hat seated to the right rear of the waggon is the reporter of the events, William King: The high point of the waggon is taken by a Mr Reynolds

30 Barking. A horse drawn sail-reaper being used on Overland Farm, c. 1900

31 A harvest gang working for Mr E. W. Snell at Darmsden Hall, Needham Market, c. 1900

32 Monks Eleigh. The driver, Mr Grainger, is showing off his Clayton & Shuttleworth steam threshing machine, *c.* 1908. They are working at Hoyland's Farm

33 Old Newton. This is the last steam contract threshing outfit to travel Suffolk. They used a Marshall, Sons & Co engine made in Gainsborough. Its number was 75077, *c.* 1909

34 The world-famous Flatford Bridge had changed little in 1890, when this photograph was taken, in the interval since Constable painted in the area some 60 years previously

35 The Mill, Buxhall. On the back of the original of this photograph is written: 'The Mill is where I used to work, the Chapel is
where I used to preach, the old house that is falling down is where
I used to live, before God called me to his work 29 years ago –
N. G. Etheridge'

36 One of the arts of the stockman, sheep dipping, seen here at
Rattlesden in 1895

37 Boxted. One of the early tractors seen here at Trucketts Farm in early November 1916. The driver is Miss Balls and her vehicle is a 'Mogul', made in the U.S.A. by the International Harvester Corporation

38 A steam driven threshing machine at Iken cliff in 1904

39 Harvesting barley at Fenn Farm (owned by Henry Fairweather) Hitcham, *c.* 1911

40 Another of the Marshall steam engines – this time an earlier model seen working at Elmswell about 1890

41 Newmarket. Four horses in line pull this timber drag down The Avenue in 1908

ROYAL OCCASIONS

The great houses of Suffolk have provided a resting place for many a royal visitor, but perhaps none more gay than the Prince of Wales later to become the Edward of our title. We see him in both of these roles as he visits the county on both formal and informal occasions.

Without a doubt, however, the outstanding royal event during the period of this work was the Diamond Jubilee of Queen Victoria in 1897. This period of her life was a sort of apotheosis, Victoria being thought to be an immortal symbol of England's greatness. Her sympathy for the common man was reflected in the great outburst of bunting and flags that greeted her fifty years as ruler of both this nation and so much of the rest of the world.

42 Saxmundham celebrating the Queen's Jubilee in 1897

43 The Suffolk Yeomanry being inspected by the Duke of York, later King George V, at Culford Park, Bury St Edmunds in 1893

44 *(overleaf)* The Royal group taken during a visit to Culford Hall, *c.* 1908. The hall was the home of the Cadogan family until it became a Methodist School in 1935

45 Abbeygate Street, Bury St Edmunds and its decorations for the Jubilee of 1887

46 The Royal shooting party when King Edward visited Culford. Included in the group are: Hon. Storor; Hon. Parker (agent to Lord Cadogan); Earl and Countess Gosford; Lady Emily Cadogan; Lord Hardwick; Countess of Cadogan; Earl Cadogan; Lord Chelsea and Hon. Gerald Cadogan; (the King is seated centre), *c.* 1905

47 The arrival of King Edward VII and Queen Alexandra outside the Abbey gate at Bury St Edmunds on Saturday 17 December 1904

GETTING ABOUT

For many a year it was true that a man travelled half a day's walk from his home and no further. Times were changing and a man's horizon was no longer limited in this way. For the rich there were the high stepping horses or even an 'Oldsmobile' or Velocipede.

Travel was no longer within the scope of the few; the stagecoach had brought some flexibility in communications and later the canal barges complemented the coach services.

Being a coastal county Suffolk had an added possibility for transport: the rivers and sea came to be used by paddle-steamers and sea-going vessels thus providing a variety of routes for both people and goods.

The industrial revolution led to the rapid growth of several towns and as their boundaries spread ever outwards it became necessary to provide a method by which the inhabitants could traverse the distance easily. The answer lay in the omnibus and later in the electric tram. Soon they were to be seen even in villages as a series of passenger routes were developed. The railway came to link the county with the rest of the nation and provide an 'export' route for goods and some people.

48 Members of the 80-strong Navigation Commissioners inspecting the River Lark, recently opened to traffic from Fordham to Bury St Edmunds. Since 1871 the powers to operate the improved parts of the river, and charge a fee for its use, had been vested in the Commissioners. Attempts to open the river up for the remaining mile from Fordham to Bury had been made unsuccessfully. This was due to some misunderstanding between the town corporation and the Commissioners. However, in 1843, 50 new Commissioners were appointed and matters improved, *c.* 1889

49 Toby Arbon driving 'Midge' and 'Billy' in the stable yard at Ickworth, *c.* 1912

50 Ready to leave Stanton is the Great Eastern Railway Omnibus.
It ran from the 'Cock' at Stanton to Bury St Edmunds and was one
of the first double-decker buses in the county, *c*. 1908

51 The 'Woolwich Belle' – the smallest of the Belle steamers, seen
on its way from Ipswich to Walton and Clacton in Essex. It was
built in 1891 by Denny, *c*. 1907

52 Horace Reynolds in his amateur role of traffic warden outside the old coaching inn, the 'Crown Hotel', at Woodbridge. He died in 1910

53 Construction work on the railway line to Felixstowe in 1877

54 Georgianna Nestling and Mrs Webber (of the
school on Market Hill, Framlingham), watched
by their pupils, on a velocipede, *c.* 1885

55 The opening of Felixstowe Town railway station in 1898

57 *(top right)* The 'Nayland Express', probably seen outside its regular stopping place of the White Hart in Nayland, *c.* 1900

56 The Ipswich 'Penny Bus'. This, like many other horse-drawn vehicles, was soon to be put out of business by the arrival of the electric trams, *c.* 1902

58 *(right)* Lowestoft Yacht basin in 1883. The Pier Pavilion, owned by the Great Eastern Railway Company, was destroyed by fire in June 1885. The twin-funnelled paddle steamer was used to tow sailing vessels to sea when calm weather or on-shore winds made putting to sea impossible under sail

60 *(above)* Awaiting the arrival of the next train on the famous Southwold Railway could, according to contemporary humorous post cards, be a full-time job! Seen here in 1902, the service operated from 1879 to 1929 and was built by Ransome and Rapier of Ipswich

61 Long Victorian clothes called for dry methods of crossing rivers. Here at Walberswick we see a chain ferry waiting to cross the river Blyth

59 *(left)* The trial trip of the new electric trams in Norwich Road, Ipswich in November, 1903

62 A pleasant way to travel was by the paddle steamers that operated out of Ipswich in the early 1900s. They are seen in this print in the 'new cut' leading to the harbour

63 *(below)* Lowestoft Harbour about 1900

64   Woodbridge station and its approaches with the River Deben in the background, *c.* 1909

65 Mr H. J. Sutton with his 'Oldsmobile' in the lanes around Waldringfield. The car previously belonged to Captain Sullivan of Melton, 1905

66 A well-known name in the area; the Moy steamers in Commercial Road, Ipswich in 1907. These steam-driven wagons could easily pull a fully laden trailer

67 Ipswich station seen just a few years after its opening nearer the town centre, *c.* 1869

68 This little loco, seen in 1902, operated a $3\frac{1}{2}$ to 4-mile length of narrow-gauge line from Barnham Station to Elveden to transport marble

69 In 1846 the Eastern Union Railway company joined Ipswich to Colchester with a 5 ft gauge line. Three years later the link to Norwich was finished. The line was later taken over by the Great Eastern Railway. The original Ipswich station was behind the cameraman taking this picture, at Croft Street, Stoke until 1 July 1860, when the tunnel, whose mouth we are now looking out of, was opened. This is the 'new' station in 1901

70 Boarding the famous train on Southwold station, *c.* 1909

71 One of the very earliest seaplanes to visit Felixstowe, *c.* 1910

72 *(right)*   A dirigible landing at Rede about 1910

73 A further expansion of the canal network can be seen under construction at Mildenhall around 1909

74 *(above)* Looking not too poorly after its forced landing at Snape is this early aeroplane, *c.* 1910

THE COMMON MAN

The basic character of the Victorians can be studied from the faces of such men as life-boatman, Robert Hook, and butcher, John Hayward. The environment has left its mark in the lines on their faces and in the steadfastness of their eyes.

This was a hard time for the ordinary man, particularly for the agricultural worker whose wages were hardly enough to support life. One outcome of this was the Agricultural Strike of 1874 which lasted during the spring and summer of that year. In the end it failed and with it an early attempt at trade unionism also ended in disgrace and bitterness.

One bright spot of the times was the beginnings of the 'pension', and we have an early photograph of the first distribution of this source of income.

Later in the period things improved a little and we can see a typical teatime scene in the Jarman household. The present Mr Jarman can be seen in the foreground – he is just a little boy. His father was the inspiration of several of the photographs in this work.

We must not forget that the 'common' man includes the 'common' woman and in the persons of the Misses Green we have examples of how they contributed to the common good.

75 *(left)* Wickhambrook on Pension Day 6 January 1908. These first pensions were restricted to those over 70 years who had been British subjects for over 20 years. They received 5 shillings a week

76 The conditions suffered by agricultural workers in Eastern England led to the formation of Agricultural unions to press for better treatment. In the spring of 1874 things came to a head with a strike and lock out of the workers. This picture shows one of their meetings in 1874

77 *(overleaf)* The young boy at the front of this group is the present Mr O. G. Jarman, whose father (the family are around him) is responsible for many of the photographs in this book. Mr Jarman tells me he was in disgrace for days after this photograph for leaving the front of his trousers undone! (*c.* 1920)

SPANTON'S
INSTANTANEOUS
PHOTOGRAPHS

THEA

NELL
GWYNNE

80 John Hayward, the butcher of Needham Market. He was dressed like this weekdays or Sundays, at work or church, *c.* 1900

79 Robert Hook (1828–1911), one of the most famous of the Lowestoft Lifeboat coxswains. He was the leader of the crews that saved over 600 lives during his time with the lifeboat service

78 *(left)* Mr Crook, the town cryer of Bury St Edmunds in 1898, is seen posting a bill advertising an exponent of the new art of instantaneous photography. Spanton, Jarman and Clarke are jointly responsible for many of the prints you see in this book

81 A school group taken at Boxford School in 1881

82 A porter of the Great Eastern Railway wearing the first uniform to be seen at Needham Market station, *c.* 1910

83 These two characters are thought to be outdoor staff of Barrow Hall, Barrow, *c.* 1900

84 Shepherd Brown of Newbourne posing in his best clothes, *c.* 1889

85 The three Misses Green outside their bake-house at Stoke-by-Nayland, *c.* 1905

87 The other great photographic family of Bury St Edmunds, the Clarkes. Here they are taking tea in the garden of their house at 7, Angel Hill, Bury

86 Sixth Suffolk Cyclist Volunteers in Burlington Road, Ipswich, *c.* 1906

88 The 'Magpie Inn' at Bury St Edmunds from the churchyard (1869). The pub was something of a 'dive' and over the years built up a reputation for being a bawdy house. When someone was murdered there the local citizens marched on the place and burned it down

89   A group of old folk having their picture taken, with the vicar
and curate, outside Lavenham Church, *c.* 1909

IN DAYS OF SAIL

The sea demands a special type of man and Suffolk has produced them in great quantity. From the days of the tall sailing ships we see packed into the harbour up to the present time this county has been a fertile place for 'sea-dogs'.

In the herring fishing fleets we have the backbone of the coastal economy. These men, who would risk the dangers of the deep to bring home their catch, are a race apart. But they are matched by the girls who followed the fish round the coasts taking employment in the fishing sheds. Typical of this breed is 'Jenny, a Scots Girl'. Theirs was the task of preparing the fish for barrels or smoking and they performed their duties in an atmosphere of wet and cold at which we can only guess.

A sailor's life is not spent all at sea – we also see him at work on shore – mending both nets and hulls.

90   Sails furled, part of the Southwold fishing fleet safely home with the herring catch. In mid stream a newer vessel, a paddle steamer, makes its way seaward

91 And we dream of days gone by . . . coast-guards and fishermen taking the air at Southwold, c. 1890

92 A brave sight; the inner harbour of Lowestoft during 1877

93 Leaving Lowestoft harbour is the sailing ship *Excel*, built in 1895 by A. Gibbs, Galmpton, for a Brixham owner. She was transferred to Lowestoft in 1902 and sold to Norway in 1910

94 After the fishing comes the repairs to both nets and boats. Southwold, *c.* 1900

96 A typical fisherman's clubhouse, 'shod' (shed). This one was on Pakefield beach, Lowestoft in 1880

95 Not the start of some strange 'land sailing race', but the very necessary drying of sails after a day's work. Southwold, *c.* 1900

98 In 1893 this was the commercial heart of Lowestoft – the Trawl Dock. In the centre of the picture is the thatched Ice House, used to store 5 cwt blocks of ice from the Norwegian fjords ready for the sailing ships to take with them to preserve their catch. During the winter months it was possible to get ice, thinner of course, from the local Broads and this was often used to supplement the imported ice

97 A photograph that one comes across so many times in Suffolk – Jenny – typical of the many Scottish fishergirls who followed the shoals of herring round the British coast. Their job was to gut and barrel the catch before it could go off, *c.* 1890

99 Barrel makers preparing the containers for the great catches of herring expected at Lowestoft, *c.* 1900

100 *(left)* Lowestoft Fish Market in 1900. From before Domesday times the town made its living from fishing, mostly herring. Much of the catch would be salted and left in piles in the fish-houses for about 50 hours. Then it would be washed and split and hung on rafters to be smoked by wood fires. Two weeks later it was ready to be packed into barrels and sent all over the country for sale.

101 While Lowestoft was the chief harbour of the herring industry it was not the only one. Here is Southwold Harbour with part of its herring fleet unloading. At one time the local fisheries were so rich that 20,000 fish a year were paid to the Lord of the Manor, *c.* 1908

HIGH DAYS AND HOLIDAYS

The simple pleasures of Victoria's England may seem unexciting to us as we look back on them but the occasional visit of a travelling bear or fair was as impressive to them as space rockets or the visit of a film personality are to us today.

To the unsophisticated countryman the rides at the travelling fair or, wonder of wonders, the news in pictures at the bioscope, were the height of excitement. Often combined with the fair were the annual agricultural shows. Here farmers could demonstrate their skills with horses or the mechanical horse harnessed to the plough. It was also a time to buy new stock and exchange news. For the younger members of the community, and for the young in heart, the churches provided an annual outing to some nearby attraction. We see waggon loads of happy villagers being pulled by steam as they depart on their day of days.

102 *(left)* Long Melford Fair in 1910. The motor car switch-back was the latest craze

103 Starters for the butter-making competition at Wickham Market, *c.* 1910

104 The Band of Hope party setting off for the annual outing to Cavendish on 4 August 1913 from Barrow

105 Getting steam up outside the 'Pickeril', Ixworth for the outing of the year, *c.* 1908

106 Ploughing teams gathering at the Market Place, Hadleigh, before taking part in the ploughing match at the local Agricultural Show, *c.* 1885

107 A celebration at Woodbridge of the centenary, in 1909, of Edward Fitzgerald (1809–83), author of *The Rubaiyat of Omar Khayyam*. Fitzgerald was born just north of here at Bredfield and lies buried at nearby Boulge

108 'All the world's news at the Bioscope Sh... calls the owner of this attraction, Mr Thur... seen in his top hat on the left. It was then at ... Melford Fair in 1908

109 Long Melford Fair and Horse Show, 1... The cottages in the top centre are 'Cor... cottages, taking their name from Sir Wil... Cordell, who founded several homes for the a...

110 Lord Kitchener talking to Boy Scout... Portman Road, Ipswich on 31 May 1911

111 The 'great frost' of 1891 left ice up to 14 inches thick on Oulton Broad. This is one way to make use of it – roasting a sheep. They kept to the edge of the Broad just in case. 12 January 1891

112 The dancing bear in the Buttermarket, Bury St Edmunds in 1900. The large staff held by the owner is not so much a whip as a means of leading the bear off into the next village

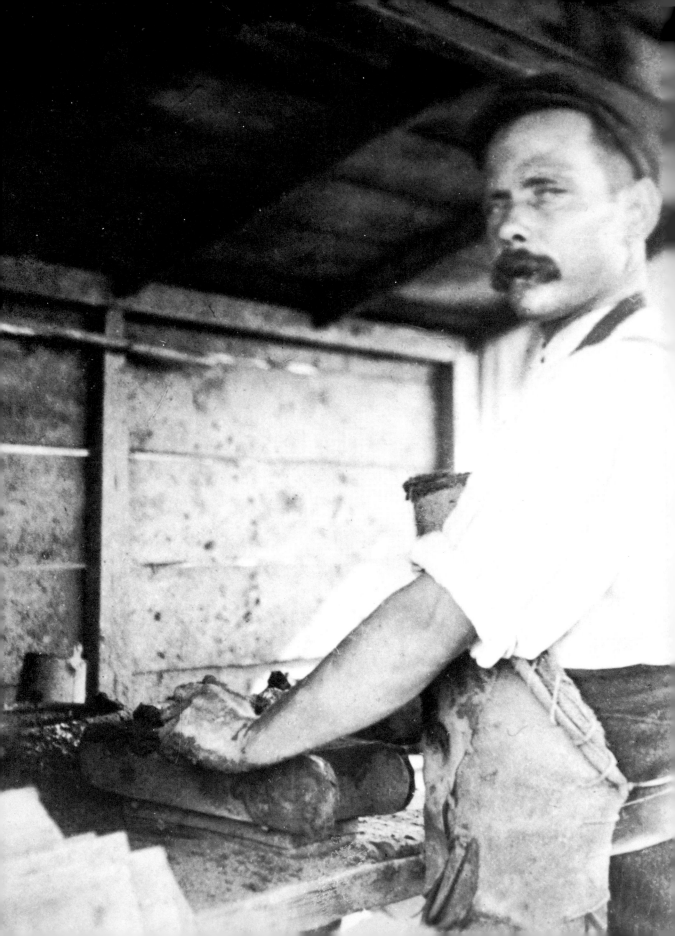

AT WORK

We have already seen man on the land and here we have a chance to look at some of the other ways in which our forebears were employed during the nineteenth century.

It is interesting to note that although the mechanical age was upon them most Victorians still worked with their hands. Nothing is more typical of the countryside than a blacksmith's forge where both horse and farm implement were catered for.

Over at Brandon a special industry grew up – the flint knappers. They worked with local material to provide gun flints, but the arrival of the percussion cap killed much of this work. So they turned to shaping flints for church building and ornamental purposes.

Men working in the heat of the Tuddingham brickworks provided part of the material for navvies who were busy constructing Felixstowe dock in 1897. Hot men need something to slake their thirst and this simple need provided employment for others. In this case the demand for beer led to the large complex of buildings at Snape where barley was malted as part of the beer-making process.

113 *(left)*   The brickworks at Tuddenham was closed in 1903; here, two years earlier, the brick is being formed by hand

114   A lost craft? Not quite. This traditional country scene of the village blacksmith at work can still be found in parts of Suffolk. This photograph was taken about 1908 in the village of Sotterley

115 Ipswich. This cabman's shelter was opened in Cornhill in January 1893. A little over two years later it had to be moved to Christchurch Park with the assistance of the corporation steam roller. (16 May 1895)

116 Felixstowe came alive when the railway arrived in 1877; soon it became clear that with this new form of transport the place had good possibilities as a port, so the construction of the dock here illustrated, began in 1897

117 *(right)* A wind pump in the Corporation Yard at Bury St Edmunds. It was built by J. W. Titt and he called it his 'Simplex'. The vanes were 60 feet across, making it one of the most modern wind engines of its time. At the time of building, 1900, it cost £550, *c.* 1911

118 *(left)* Much of the barley that was grown on the eastern side of Suffolk must have found its way to these famous Maltings at Snape. We see them around 1900. Now the Maltings are better known as the setting for the Aldburgh Festival

119 The construction of the Bury St Edmunds sewage works at West Stow in 1894. The detritus tank system was used to clear the sewage. In 1971 a new complex was built on another site

120 Workmen building the Harbour Bridge, Lowestoft, 1897

121 *(right)* This huge structure is a water wheel and it was made in Bury St Edmunds by Joseph Bridge in his Victoria Street works, *c.* 1899

122 Brandon flint knappers, showing the skilled craft of fitting flints into old weapons, *c.* 1910

124 *(right)* Stoke Windmill. Built on land in the 'waste' of the Manor of Stoke, it is mentioned in the oldest preserved records of the Parish, the overseers' accounts of 1746. We see it in 1884, some three years before it finally ended its career. Standing next to it is Mr Goodchild, the last owner, who is reputed to have put the mill's lack of profitability down to the fact that so many houses had been built locally that they stopped the wind reaching his sails

123 Mr Kerry is seen by his new Aveling & Porter 10 ton steam roller. It was photographed in Westgate Street, Bury St Edmunds in 1911

125 Dan Whitman is seen working at the furnace of the brickworks in Tuddenham in 1900

126 Billy Cooper, once well known as a coalman in Lowestoft, with his cart and two donkeys, Obadiah and Malachi, on the west side of London Road North. Billy was susceptible to a quick doze. Local boys used sometimes to untie his donkeys and hide them from him! (*c.* 1879)

DISASTER

We all tend to look back with nostalgia to the 'good old days'. As we have seen elsewhere in this book they were not always so good for everyone. Each age has its share of trouble and disaster and the Victorians were no exception. Our illustrations show regional, local and personal troubles. The traction engine killing its driver as it falls into the river and the unexpected fall of a church tower are but two of the many troubles that beset people.

Assuming larger significance was the ever-present greed of the sea as it ate into Suffolk's coastline, pulling land, houses and finally even villages into its dark depths.

In 1871 the gunpowder factory at Stowmarket exploded killing some 23 people, an event remembered to this day by the locals.

Six years later it was flood water that provided the source of worry as it overan both town and country.

127 *(left)*   One way to keep dry during the floods of Lowestoft in 1897. This scene, typical of many others is in Tonning Street

128   'Without knocking too . . .' Bury St Edmunds, 21 April 1897

129 The remains of the south-west tower of All Saints church, Stanton, after its sudden collapse on 5 March 1906. It has never been re-built

130 The temporary home of the church bell after its tower had fallen down. All Saints Church, Stanton, 1906

131   The driver of this traction engine, Thomas Newell, was killed at Fornham bridge on 16 June 1890. He was travelling with his steerer (Mr A. Hunt, who escaped injury) when they came to the bridge. Being a stranger to the district the driver asked a local if he had ever seen an engine cross the bridge. The local replied that he had and with that they drove the traction engine onto the bridge and it gave way. At the inquest their informant said they never asked him if the bridge was safe (which he knew it was not) but if he had seen an engine cross it (which he had!)

132 Locals will tell you that half of Southwold already lies under the sea. Here we catch the events of 2 October 1905 when yet another piece of the coast was lost to the waves

133 Lowestoft: Viewing the devastation on the cliffs as yet another cottage (Pakefield) falls into the sea during October 1905. Over a hundred others have followed it during this century

134 During the nineteenth century the gun-cotton and cordite industry was established in Stowmarket. In August 1871 there was a terrible explosion and the factory was almost totally destroyed. Twenty-three people were killed and several more injured. The explosion rocked homes for miles around and broke thousands of windows

135 The Ipswich flood of July 1902. Pumping out cellars in Brook Street

136 The Layham water mill after its destruction by fire, *c.* 1900

IN PUBLIC SERVICE

The unsung heroes of any age are those whose works add to the fullness of all our lives but of whom we usually hear very little. In this section we take the opportunity to put this a little to rights as we picture the men and women in public service and the way they looked and worked.

Postmen who by foot and cycle covered the county with their mail; firemen with simple equipment always ready to fight that great enemy of the thatched home.

We also have the rare chance to look back at the medical services and the people who ran them. Doctors and nurses care for children in both East and West Suffolk hospitals, and pose for the group photo!

137 Nurses and doctor of the East Suffolk Hospital, Ipswich, *c.* 1867

138 The Hopton fire engine and crew, *c.* 1910?

139 *(overleaf)* A children's ward at the East Suffolk Hospital, Ipswich, *c.* 1870

140 An operation in progress at the West Suffolk General Hospital, Bury St Edmunds, *c.* 1910

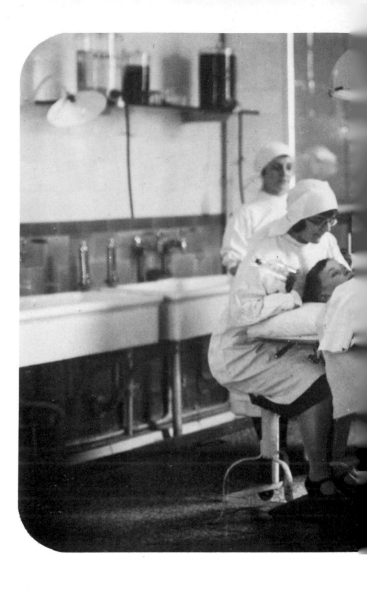

141 Postmen ready to set off on the morning round, outside the post office at Woodbridge, *c.* 1910

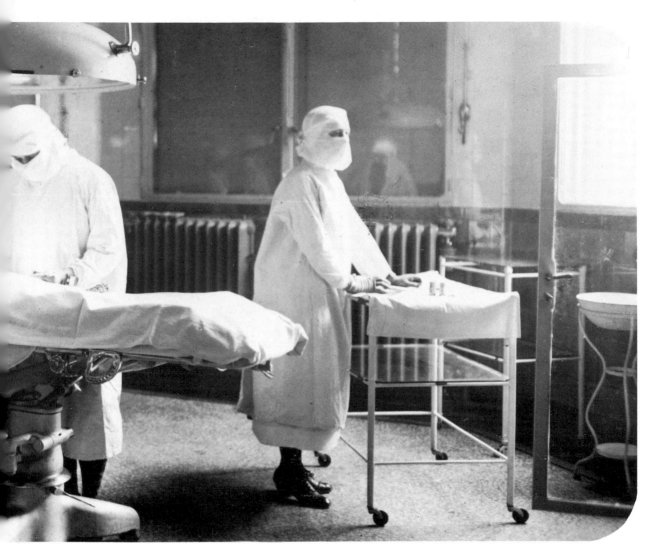

SPORTS, PASTIMES AND SEASIDE

A donkey ride for the kids, a quiet stroll for the adults or a dip in the sea for all are pleasures that we share with our forebears. It is interesting to note that it was really only during the early years of Victoria's reign that the habit of going to the seaside for a holiday got under way. I think you will agree that it is a wonder it ever caught on at all when we look at the swimsuits they had to wear and realise the trouble they had to go to just to get changed. Perhaps the oldest of our village sports are cricket and quoits, with tennis arriving later. Quoits dates from around 1500 and has the advantage over other sports in that a 'team' can consist of any number of players – a great pub game.

With the numerous rivers and lakes in the county it is only to be expected that sailing and rowing should figure largely in the list of pastimes, but few can have participated in the latest craze of the age, the motor gymkhana.

142   Kirkley Cliffs, Lowestoft in 1900. The fore-ground was to be taken up by the first Claremont Pier in 1901 and this became the calling point for the Thames to Great Yarmouth passenger steamers

143   Footman Pretty's cricket team of 1863. They were an Ipswich XI

144 Sailing in the dock basin at Ipswich, *c.* 1902

145 Woolpit. Its name reminds us of the origin of the place – the pits were then to trap wolves. The present hunt, seen outside the 'Old Commercial Inn' in about 1896, is seeking the more traditional fox

146 The Brockford Quoits players outside the pub – after a famous victory? (*c.* 1900)

147 On the river Deben, Waldringfield, *c.* 1885

148 Motor Gymkhana at Drinkstone, *c.* 1910

149 Mixed cricket at 'The Laurels', the home of George Simpson in Stonham Aspal, *c.* 1907

150 Mixed doubles at the tennis tournament at Aldeburgh in 1908

151   Gorleston Pier, *c.* 1900

152   The Asses Stand on Lowestoft South Beach, 1893

153 A bathing machine near the then recently opened Claremont
Pier (1902). The first bathing machines reached Lowestoft in 1768,
and local bye-laws of 1888 laid down that male and female bathers
must be a minimum of 100 yards apart

154   Felixstowe; the bay looking east, *c*. 1910

155   Pony rides on Lowestoft beach, *c*. 1884. The harbour is off to the left.

156 The donkey ride on Lowestoft's South
Beach in about 1880

157 Felixstowe beach about 1910

ROUND ABOUT SUFFOLK

This farewell chapter provides a scenic montage of the county as it will never be seen again. Look at the quiet village lanes, free of traffic, where man and animal could wander in freedom. It was a time when neighbours could while away the time of day on the door-steps and still be heard, or cross the road and join in with the Salvation Army in streetside worship without the danger of causing an obstruction to traffic.

We can also see the uninhibited excitement when the first trains started running in the county.

This juxtaposition of the eternal quality of nature and the developing brashness of man is perhaps the final picture of an age that links rural Suffolk with the modern age.

158 *(left)*   Delivering milk in New Street, Wood-bridge, *c.* 1900

159   The High Street, Lowestoft, 1897. Mr Rand, the bearded postman, is approaching the Parish Rectory – the tall building on the right. This view has vanished with the widening of the road

160   Glemsford, *c.* 1900. 'The Plough Inn', and across the road is a 'used' cart lot!

The Green Wormeford

161 Church Street, Wangford, *c.* 1900

162 The Thorofare (main street) Halesworth, *c.* 1909

163 Haverhill: the High Street and Market Street in *c.* 1884

164 Needham Market, 1895. These houses were pulled down in 1901 to make way for a Wesleyan Chapel

165 The 'Swan Inn', Lavenham, seen on the right in the late 1860s, has part of its structure going back to 1300. It was in Lavenham that Jane Taylor wrote her famous children's poem 'Twinkle, Twinkle, little star.'

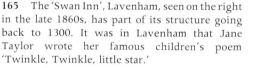

166 The New Bridge in Lowestoft, 1897. For some 20 minutes both the old and the new bridge operated together. Then the old one, on the right, closed for good after 60 years of service (1837–97). Yet another 'new bridge' is now (1972), operating as a replacement for the one shown here

167   Beccles, once famous for herrings, is now better known for its printing works. In 1749 the then curate of Beccles married the daughter of the rector of nearby Barsham – their son was Horatio Nelson. (c. 1904)

168   Alderton High Street, c. 1904

169 A foot wide and eight feet long, this sand writing table was used for many years in the parish school to teach reading and writing. Pen and paper were too expensive! It now stands in Dennington Church. Next to it is 'Peter's Pence Box'; cut from solid oak it is said to be thief proof – opening one lock closes yet another, c. 1900

170 The Salvation Army holding a meeting at Woodbridge in 1898